Seeing Both Sides

Field Trips,
Yes or No

Kevin Walker

Rourke
Educational Media

rourkeeducationalmedia.com

Before Reading:

Building Academic Vocabulary and Background Knowledge

Before reading a book, it is important to tap into what your child or students already know about the topic. This will help them develop their vocabulary, increase their reading comprehension, and make connections across the curriculum.

1. *Look at the cover of the book. What will this book be about?*
2. *What do you already know about the topic?*
3. *Let's study the Table of Contents. What will you learn about in the book's chapters?*
4. *What would you like to learn about this topic? Do you think you might learn about it from this book? Why or why not?*
5. *Use a reading journal to write about your knowledge of this topic. Record what you already know about the topic and what you hope to learn about the topic.*
6. *Read the book.*
7. *In your reading journal, record what you learned about the topic and your response to the book.*
8. *After reading the book complete the activities below.*

Content Area Vocabulary
Read the list. What do these words mean?

alternative
critical
disrupt
exploration
fascinate
inspiration
liability
majesty
memorable
virtual

After Reading:

Comprehension and Extension Activity

After reading the book, work on the following questions with your child or students in order to check their level of reading comprehension and content mastery.

1. *What is an opinion? (Summarize)*
2. *How do personal experiences shape someone's opinion? (Infer)*
3. *What are some ways not listed in the book that field trips benefit students? (Asking questions)*
4. *What is the most interesting place you've visited on a field trip? (Text to self connection)*
5. *Why do some schools have to reduce the number of field trips students take? (Asking questions)*

Extension Activity
If you could go anywhere in the world on a field trip, where would you go? Research the place you chose and create a presentation about it to take your class on a virtual field trip!

Table of Contents

Taking Sides

What do you think about school field trips? Are they fun and educational? Or are they boring and a waste of time and money?

Many people have opinions on field trips. Answering those questions can help you form one, too.

You already know all about opinions. You probably have one about the best color, sport, or music. You show your opinion about food every time you pass over broccoli to take a bite of macaroni and cheese!

However, explaining your opinion on a topic such as field trips means researching facts and details about the issue, as well as thinking about your own experiences.

Field Trips? Yes, Please!

Schools plan field trips to see places they discussed in class. That's because while teachers try hard to make every subject interesting, it's easier to **fascinate** students when they see something with their own eyes.

Field trips give students a day away from the classroom that is not only educational, but often **memorable**.

Reality ✓

Students who take field trips develop stronger thinking skills and are more tolerant of others, experts say.

Field trips fall into a handful of categories. They are usually historic places, art museums, museums of science and natural history, zoos and parks, or wildlife areas.

Field trips are better than just visiting a place with your family because what you experience is designed to help you understand a topic you studied in class. You can take notes while you are there and discuss them in the classroom with your teacher and fellow students.

Zoos are visited by people all the time. But isn't it even more interesting when there is someone there who can tell you more about the animals?

Zookeepers or veterinarians can answer all your questions and teach you more about the animals you think are interesting.

No picture can capture the **majesty** of a black bear quite like seeing one in person. Plus, where else could you see a bear, boa constrictor, or rhinoceros without worrying about your safety?

Reality ✓

Many zoos offer animal encounters for large groups of students, which can range from touching a sea turtle to hand-feeding a panda bear.

Natural wildlife parks also are interesting because you see animals in their natural environment. Of course, the environment depends on where you live, but visiting a swamp, desert, mountain, lake, or river can make the facts you learned in a textbook come alive.

Science museums give students the opportunity to see exhibits or films in a planetarium that can help you understand the vastness of space or how planets move around the sun.

Some even have dinosaur fossil specimens. Just seeing a Tyrannosaurus Rex is worth riding a bus to the museum!

Reality ✓

The most complete Tyrannosaurus Rex specimen is "Sue" at the Field Museum of Natural History in Chicago, Illinois.

Art museums give students a chance to learn about art movements, such as the Impressionist and Surrealist periods, when artists worked together to try to change how people viewed the world.

There is also performance art, where students can see dancers or acrobats live on stage, and musical performances, such as the local symphony.

Many memorable field trips are to historical sites, such as battleships, old forts, important buildings and aircraft. Students may complain in class that history is boring, but few are bored climbing around a real battleship.

There are other benefits to field trips, too. They help develop **critical** thinking skills. This helps students evaluate and analyze something and come up with their own opinion.

Another benefit of field trips is appreciation of culture. This is especially true for visits to art museums, where you learn about history through art and the ways artists reacted to historical events.

Field trips may also lead to being a better student. One study found students who went on field trips had better grades and were more likely to graduate high school and college.

Field trips also allow everyone to participate. Some students come from families who may not have enough money to take their children to museums or historical sites.

Field trips also help students identify areas of interest. For example, a trip to the science museum could spark an interest in space **exploration**. Those who visit a zoo might become interested in working with animals. Young artists might find **inspiration** on the walls of the local art museum.

When you think about it, it's easy to see how field trips are an important part of every school year.

Field Trips? No Way!

Field trips may sound good when you think about the places you could go, but that's only if you are interested in those places. What if you're not?

Also, one student can **disrupt** and ruin a field trip by acting out, making it a bad day for all the teachers and students, too.

Reality ✓

Some schools have students sign a field trip behavior contract, which outlines the rules they must follow on field trips.

There is no way for teachers to pick a place everyone will
like. Students have many different interests. Not everyone
will like the field trip choice. That means that even before you
leave, at least some students will wish they weren't going.

Field trips also are hard on schools. Planning field trips takes time that teachers could spend actually teaching or preparing for class.

Some things teachers and school officials need for school trips include: transportation back and forth, chaperones, food for all the students, and coming up with **alternative** plans in case it rains.

Math equations on chalkboard:

$$0 + 2 = 7$$
$$6 + 10 = 16$$
$$6 + 3 = 9$$
$$12 - 7 = 5$$
$$1 - 7 = 4$$
$$9 + 12 = 21$$
$$21 - 14 = 7$$
$$8 + 16 = 24$$

Reality ✓

Schools sometimes get in trouble because of places they take students on field trips. For example, religious-themed school trips or visiting places where there were reenactments of slavery.

They must also have signed permission slips from every parent and know all the allergies students have and make sure they take medicine. They also need emergency contacts because sometimes accidents happen on field trips.

All of this costs schools money. They have to get **liability** insurance to cover all students in case of accidents.

Some schools don't have enough money to pay for necessary classroom supplies. How can they spend money taking a busload of students to an art museum when they cannot afford basic items?

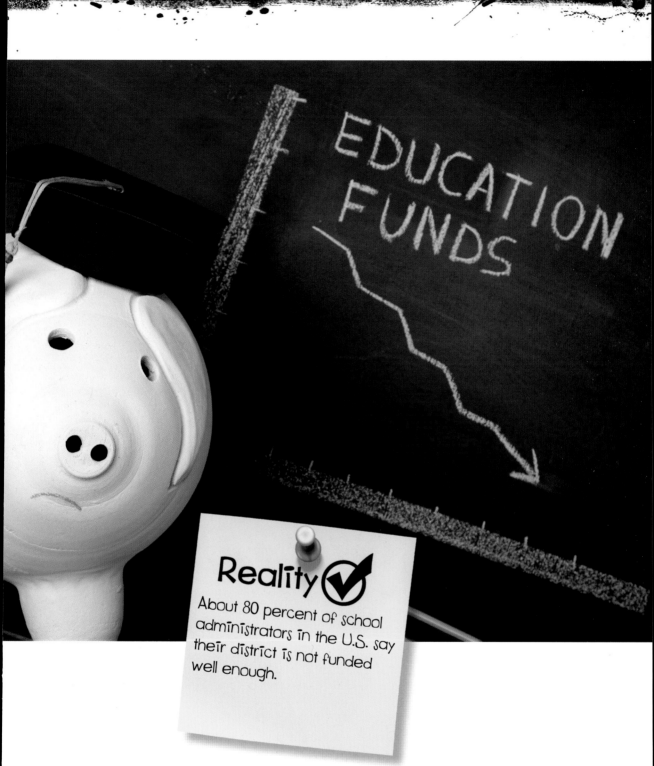

Reality ✓

About 80 percent of school administrators in the U.S. say their district is not funded well enough.

This is why many schools are now cutting field trips, along with some types of classes. It's hard to pay for field trips when the schools have less and less money.

There is another way to give students the experience of going on a field trip that is safe and does not cost much. Thanks to the Internet, some schools do **virtual** field trips where they look at images on computer screens right from the classroom.

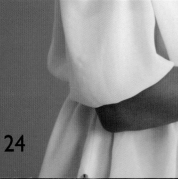

Virtual field trips are an alternative to costly, time-consuming field trips. This idea not only saves the school money, but some students like it better. Many students feel that a virtual field trip is better than boarding a school bus and going to a museum and listening to a boring speech about each of the exhibits.

Reality ✓

One of the most popular virtual tours is offered by the Smithsonian Museum in Washington, D.C., where students can tour the whole museum in a 360-degree environment.

Another reason why a virtual field trip is better than a regular field trip is that you can take your time and not be rushed. There's no time wasted driving back and forth, and organizing into groups, like on a regular field trip. This allows more time to focus on the place they're learning about. All you need is an Internet connection!

School fields trip are far more trouble than they are worth, especially when an Internet connection and a big screen can give students a similar experience without all the potential problems of traditional field trips.

Your Turn

Now that you have read arguments for and against field trips, which one do you agree with more? Did both sides present their opinion with research, facts, and examples?

Using the book as a model, write your own opinion paper. Make sure to use facts, details, and examples. You can also add experiences from your own life that support your position.

Telling Your Side: Writing Opinion Pieces

- Tell your opinion first. Use phrases such as:
- *I like* _____.
- *I think* ____.
- _____ *is the best* _____.
- Give multiple reasons to support your opinion. Use facts and relevant information instead of stating your feelings.
- Use the words *and*, *because*, and *also* to connect your opinion to your reasons.
- Clarify or explain your facts by using the phrases *for example* or *such as*.
- Compare your opinion to a different opinion. Then point out reasons that your opinion is better. You can use phrases such as:
- *Some people think*_____, *but I disagree because*

  _____.
- _____ *is better than* _____ *because* _____.
- Give examples of positive outcomes if the reader agrees with your opinion. For example, you can use the phrase, *If*

  _____ *then* _____.
- Use a personal story about your own experiences with your topic. For example, if you are writing about your opinion on after-school sports, you can write about your own experiences with after-school sports activities.
- Finish your opinion piece with a strong conclusion that highlights your strongest arguments. Restate your opinion so your reader remembers how you feel.

Glossary

alternative (awl-TUR-nuh-tiv): a choice that is not the usual one

critical (KRIT-i-kuhl): expressing a negative opinion or finding fault

disrupt (dis-RUHPT): to disturb or interrupt something that is happening

exploration (ek-spluh-RAY-shuhn): the act of studying an unknown thing or place

fascinate (FAS-uh-nate): to attract and hold the attention of

inspiration (in-spuh-RAY-shun): something that inspires someone, such as a person, event, or idea

liability (lye-uh-BIL-i-tee): responsibility

majesty (MAJ-i-stee): impressive or dignified

memorable (MEM-ur-uh-buhl): worth remembering, or easy to remember because of some special feature

virtual (VUR-choo-uhl): made to seem like the real thing

Index

Show What You Know

1. What kind of places are typically visited on school field trips?

2. Name two reasons students might feel negatively about field trips?

3. What is the reason some school districts cut field trips?

4. What museum is the home for "Sue," the most complete Tyrannosaurus Rex specimen?

5. What museum has one of the most popular virtual tours?

Websites to Visit

www.debate.org/opinions/should-schools-have-more-field-trips
www.nps.gov/index.htm
www.studygs.net/wrtstr4.htm

About the Author

Kevin Walker is a writer, editor, and father who lives in Texas, but he still prefers sneakers to cowboy boots. He thinks the best way to form an opinion is to carefully consider both sides of the issue. But his favorite color is blue and no one can change his mind about that.

Meet The Author!
www.meetREMauthors.com

© 2016 Rourke Educational Media

www.rourkeeducationalmedia.com

PHOTO CREDITS: Cover (top): ©Kletr; cover (Bottom): ©Patrick Foto; page 1: ©Mike Watson; page 3, 9: ©Susan Chiang; page 4 (left): ©canyons; page 4 (left): ©tacar; page 5: ©Steve Debenport; page 6, 26: ©Christopher Futcher; page 7: ©Darrell Young; page 8: ©Pamela Albin Moore; page 10: ©tobiasjo; page 10, 18, 19, 23: ©loops7; page 11: ©ShootingAmerica; page 12: ©Ginosphotos; page 13: ©IgorBulgarin; page 14: ©bondon22; page 15: ©Leesniderphotoimages; page 16: ©IPGGutenbergUKLtd; page 17: ©LindaMoon; page 18: ©Solstock; page 19: ©skynesher; page 20, 21: ©svetikd; page 22: ©pinstock; page 23: ©Rodolfo Arguedas; page 27: ©Shaun_lowe; page 28: ©MachineHeadz; page 29: ©Sezeryadigar

Edited by: Keli Sipperley

Cover design by: Rhea Magaro
Interior design by: Tara Raymo

Library of Congress PCN Data

Field Trips, Yes or No / Kevin Walker
  (Seeing Both Sides)
   ISBN 978-1-68191-387-2 (hard cover)
   ISBN 978-1-68191-429-9 (soft cover)
   ISBN 978-1-68191-469-5 (e-Book)
Library of Congress Control Number: 2015951555

Also Available as:

Printed in the United States of America, North Mankato, Minnesota